YOU CAN DRAW IT!
AIRCRAFT

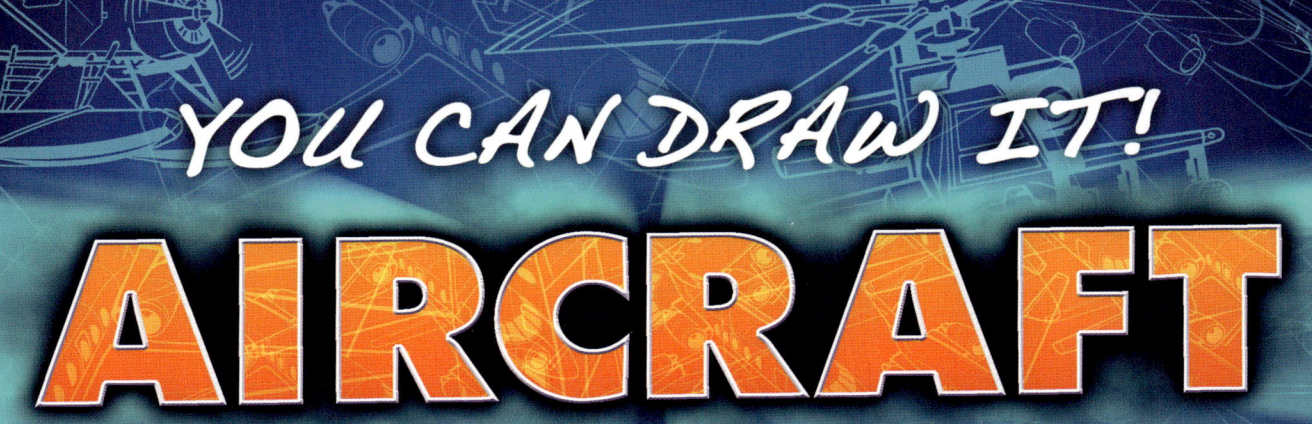

WRITTEN BY JON EPPARD
ILLUSTRATED BY STEVE PORTER

BELLWETHER MEDIA • MINNEAPOLIS, MN

This edition first published in 2013 by Bellwether Media, Inc.

No part of this publication may be reproduced in whole or in part without written permission of the publisher. For information regarding permission, write to Bellwether Media, Inc., Attention: Permissions Department, 5357 Penn Avenue South, Minneapolis, MN 55419.

Library of Congress Cataloging-in-Publication Data

Eppard, Jon.
 Aircraft / by Jon Eppard.
     pages cm – (You can draw it!)
 Includes bibliographical references and index.
 Summary: "Information accompanies step-by-step instructions on how to draw aircraft. The text level and subject matter is intended for students in grades 3 through 7"–Provided by publisher.
 ISBN 978-1-60014-808-8 (hardcover : alk. paper) – ISBN 978-1-60014-853-8 (pbk. : alk. paper)
  1. Aeronautics in art–Juvenile literature. 2. Airplanes in art–Juvenile literature. 3. Drawing–Technique–Juvenile literature. I. Title.
 NC825.A4E67 2012
 743'.89629133–dc23
                                      2012018245

Text copyright © 2013 by Bellwether Media, Inc. PILOT, EXPRESS, and associated logos are trademarks and/or registered trademarks of Bellwether Media, Inc. SCHOLASTIC, CHILDREN'S PRESS, and associated logos are trademarks and/or registered trademarks of Scholastic Inc.

Printed in the United States of America, North Mankato, MN.

TABLE OF CONTENTS

Aircraft! 4
F-22 Raptor 6
Jayhawk Helicopter 8
Hot Air Balloon 10
Stunt Plane 12
Airbus A380 14
Seaplane 16
Learjet 18
Apache Helicopter 20
Glossary 22
To Learn More 23
Index 24

AIRCRAFT!

People can travel through the sky in many different ways. Passenger jets, helicopters, and even hot air balloons transport people from place to place. Fighter planes and attack helicopters serve the military around the world. Other aircraft perform stunts and entertain audiences at air shows.

DRAWING FROM PHOTOS IS A GREAT PLACE TO START. WORK YOUR WAY UP TO DRAWING FROM MEMORY OR YOUR IMAGINATION.

Before you begin drawing, you will need a few basic supplies.

PAPER

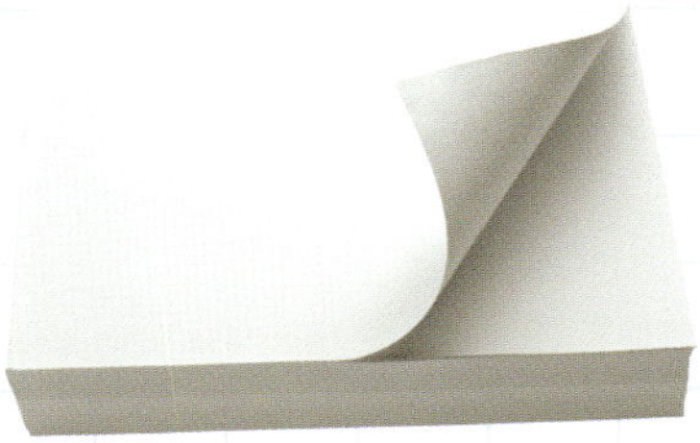

DRAWING PENCILS

BLACK INK PEN

2B OR NOT 2B?

NOT ALL DRAWING PENCILS ARE THE SAME. "B" PENCILS ARE SOFTER, MAKE DARKER MARKS, AND SMUDGE EASILY. "H" PENCILS ARE HARDER, MAKE LIGHTER MARKS, AND DON'T SMUDGE VERY MUCH AT ALL.

COLORED PENCILS
(ALL DRAWINGS IN THIS BOOK WERE FINISHED WITH COLORED PENCILS.)

ERASER

PENCIL SHARPENER

F-22 Raptor
Advanced Jet Fighter

One of the most advanced jet fighters in the world, the F-22 Raptor can dominate the sky. The aircraft is equipped with **stealth** technology to hide it from enemy **radar**. Bombs, **missiles**, and a large gun help it destroy enemy bases and vehicles. If an enemy fighter engages a Raptor, the F-22 is sure to win the **dogfight**!

BREAK IT DOWN

JUST ABOUT ANY SUBJECT YOU'RE DRAWING CAN BE BROKEN DOWN INTO SMALLER PARTS. LOOK FOR CIRCLES, OVALS, SQUARES, AND OTHER BASIC SHAPES THAT CAN HELP BUILD YOUR DRAWING.

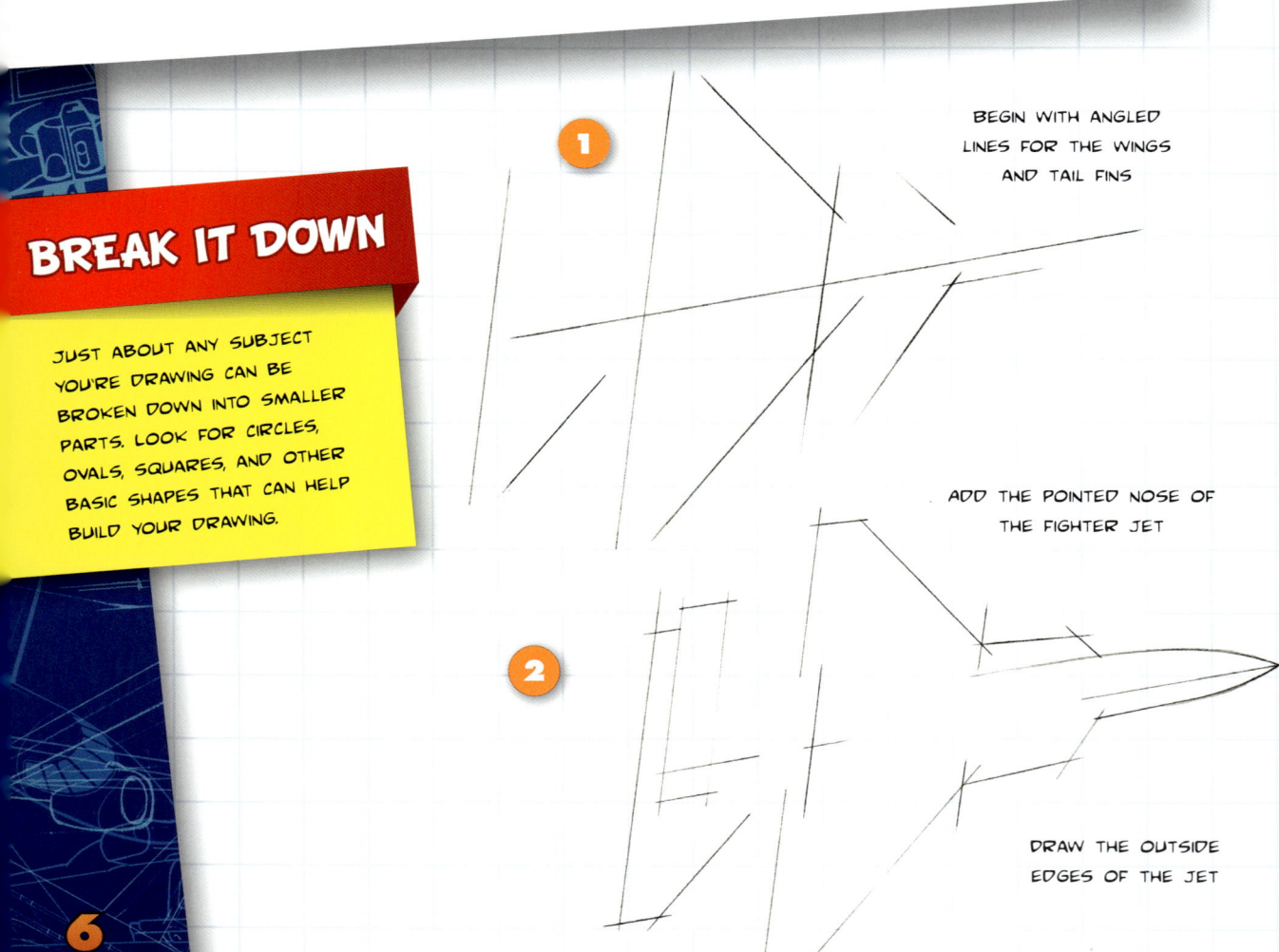

1. BEGIN WITH ANGLED LINES FOR THE WINGS AND TAIL FINS

2. ADD THE POINTED NOSE OF THE FIGHTER JET

DRAW THE OUTSIDE EDGES OF THE JET

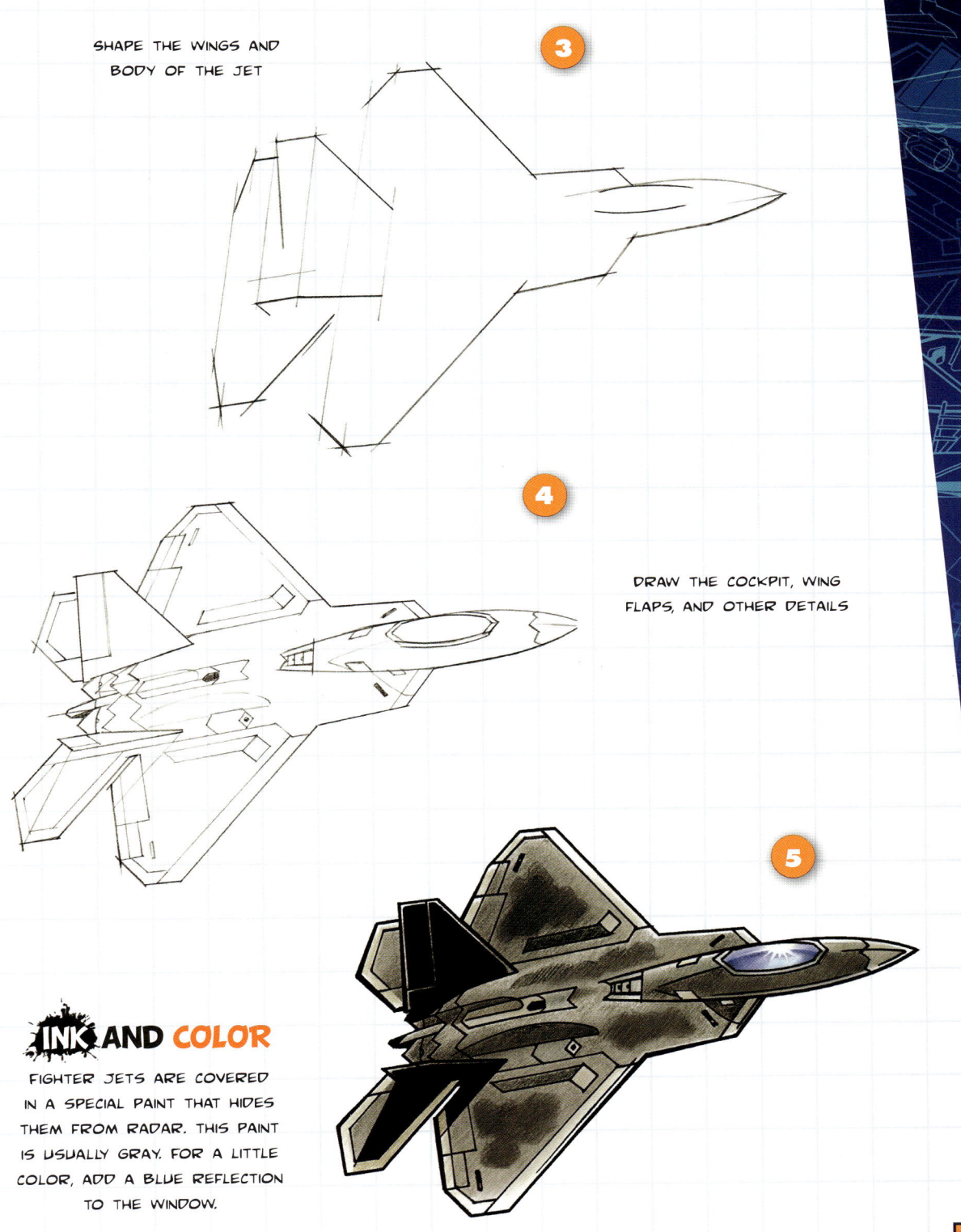

Jayhawk Helicopter
Rescue Helicopter

Braving violent storms, United States Coast Guard helicopters fly out to sea to rescue victims of shipwrecks and other disasters. The Jayhawk is most famous for these search-and-rescue missions. The helicopter has a **hoist** to pull victims out of the water to safety. For people stranded at sea, the Jayhawk is a welcome sight.

LIGHT TO DARK

BEGIN YOUR DRAWING WITH VERY LIGHT LINES. SLOWLY BUILD UP TO DARK LINES AS YOU REACH THE FINAL STEPS. THIS WILL ALLOW FOR EASY CORRECTION OF MISTAKES.

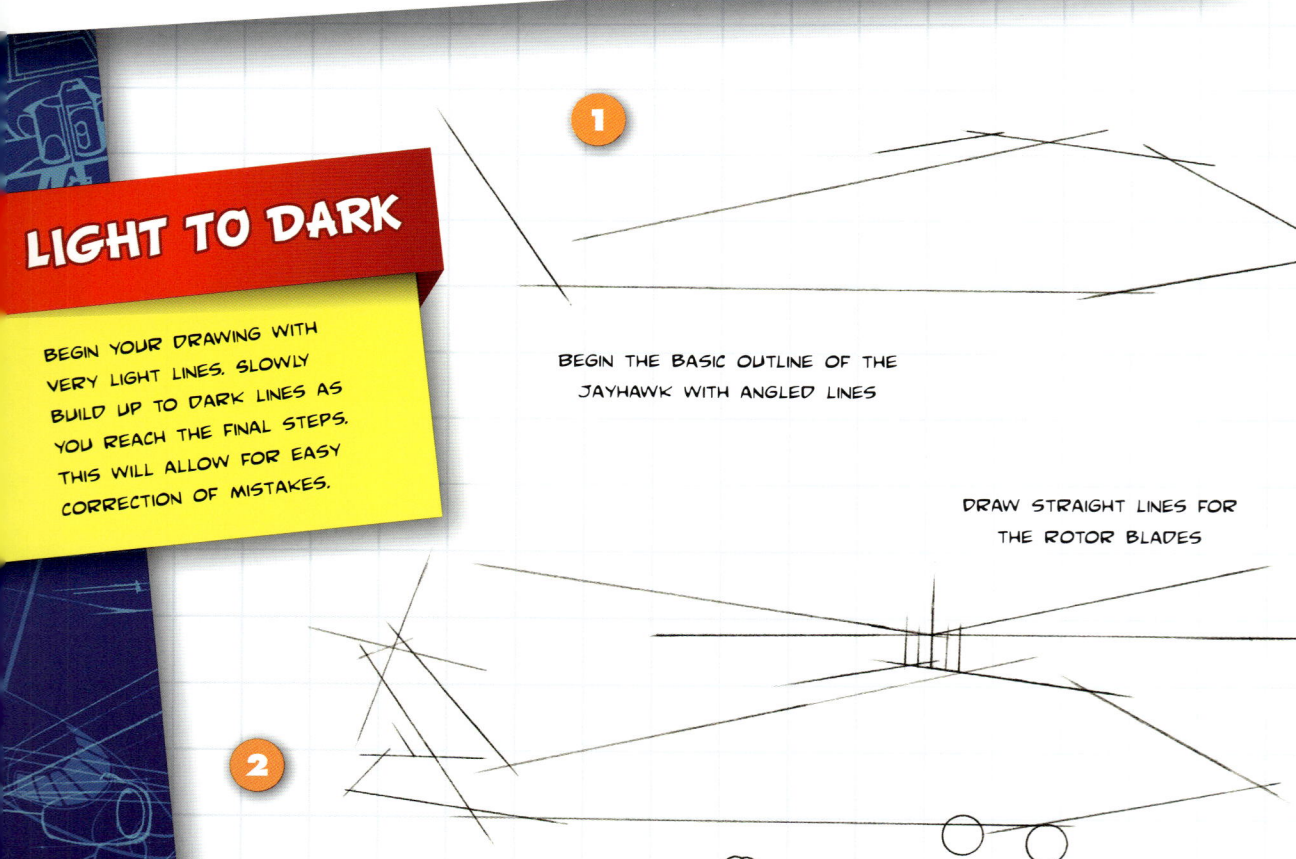

1. BEGIN THE BASIC OUTLINE OF THE JAYHAWK WITH ANGLED LINES

   DRAW STRAIGHT LINES FOR THE ROTOR BLADES

2. LIGHTLY ADD THE TAIL FIN AND TAIL ROTOR

   ADD CIRCLES FOR THE WHEELS

ROUND THE OUTER EDGES
OF THE HELICOPTER

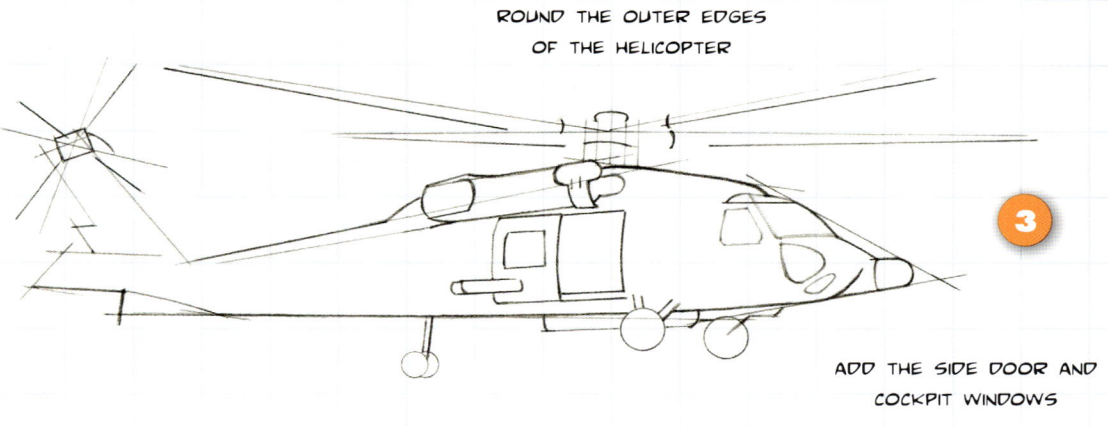

ADD THE SIDE DOOR AND
COCKPIT WINDOWS

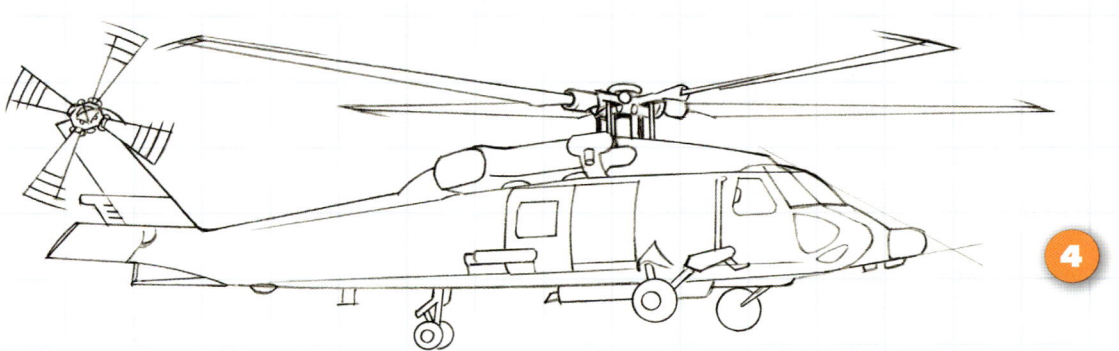

ADD DETAIL TO THE MAIN ROTOR,
TAIL ROTOR, AND WHEELS

INK AND COLOR

COLOR THE JAYHAWK REDDISH ORANGE
AND WHITE. THESE ARE TRADITIONAL
COAST GUARD COLORS.

Hot Air Balloon
Flying Parachute

In the late 1700s, two brothers used hot air to lift a sheep, duck, and rooster off the ground in France. Since then, hot air balloons have been used for sightseeing, transport, and military **recon**. Unlike early models, modern hot air balloons have an onboard heat source and are able to stay in the air for up to weeks at a time. A few brave pilots have even flown around the world!

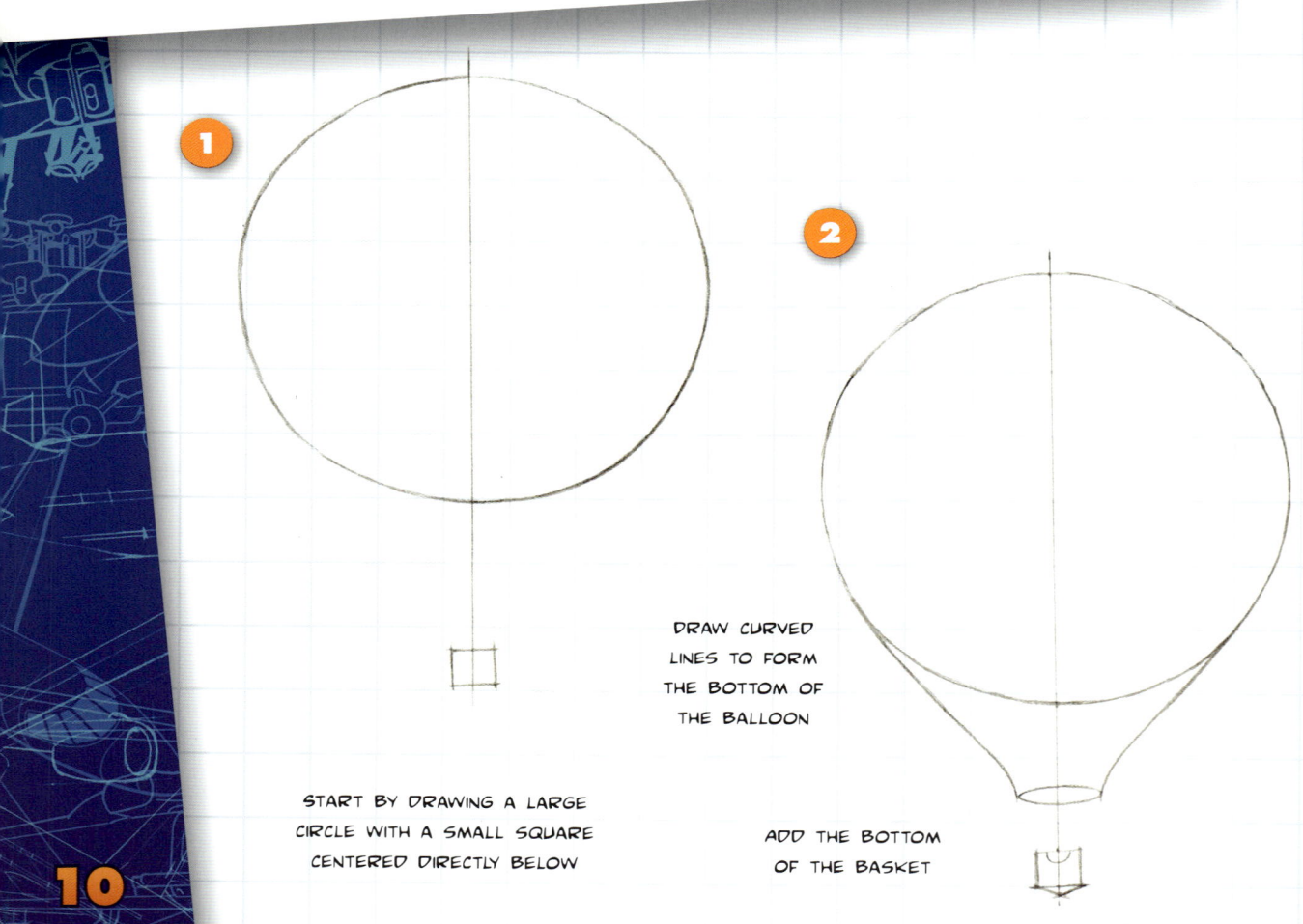

1. START BY DRAWING A LARGE CIRCLE WITH A SMALL SQUARE CENTERED DIRECTLY BELOW

2. DRAW CURVED LINES TO FORM THE BOTTOM OF THE BALLOON

ADD THE BOTTOM OF THE BASKET

Stunt Plane
Spinning Machine

Stunt planes participate in the sport of **aerobatics**. The small, **maneuverable** planes perform rolls, loops, and spins to the amazement of crowds watching from below. Pilots often enter competitions to show their skills in front of judges. The pilot with the best moves wins!

USE YOUR ARM

Draw with your whole arm, not just your wrist and fingers.

1. START WITH ANGLED LINES FOR THE BODY AND WINGS

2. ADD THE TAIL FIN

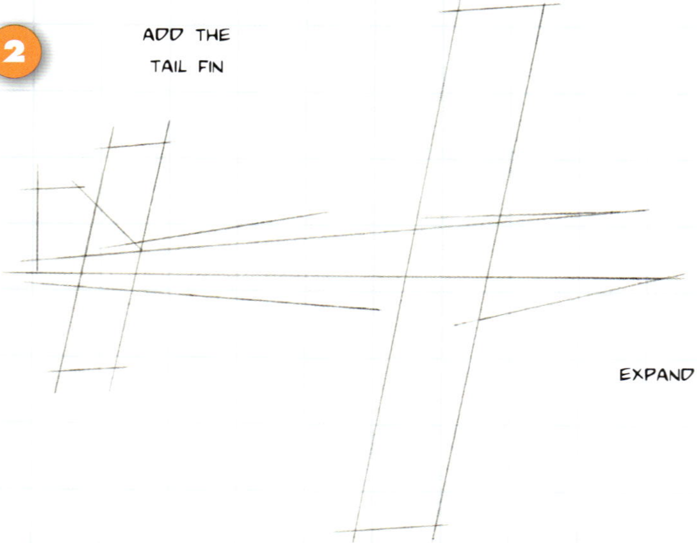

EXPAND THE BODY

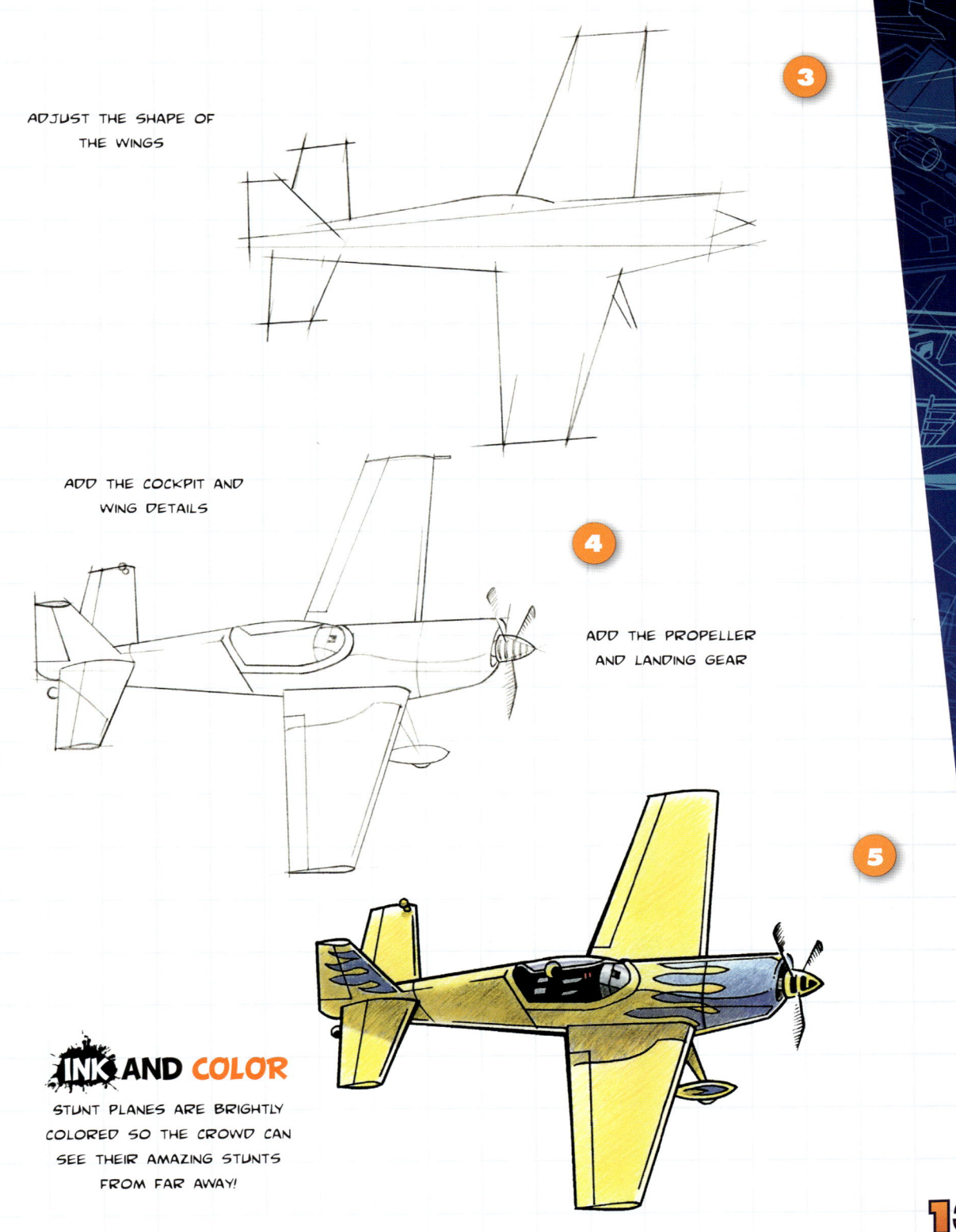

Airbus A380
Largest Passenger Airliner

The Airbus A380 is the world's largest **passenger airliner**. With a range of 9,600 miles (15,400 kilometers), an Airbus can fly to almost any major city in the world without refueling. Some airports have had to remodel to allow the 260-foot (80-meter) wingspan to fit into their **gates**!

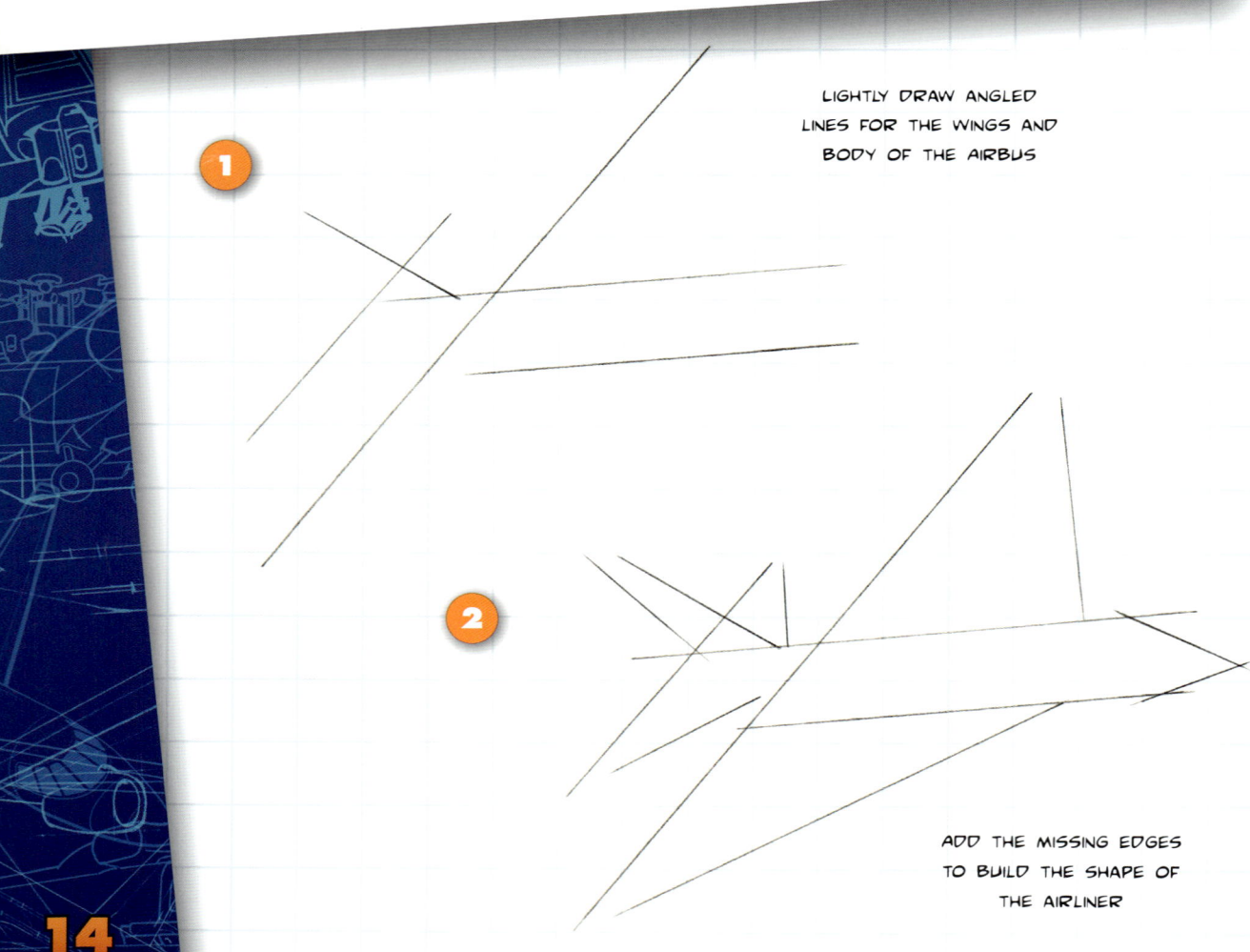

1. LIGHTLY DRAW ANGLED LINES FOR THE WINGS AND BODY OF THE AIRBUS

2. ADD THE MISSING EDGES TO BUILD THE SHAPE OF THE AIRLINER

DRAW THE FOUR ENGINES BELOW THE WINGS

3

ROUND THE FRONT EDGE OF THE AIRBUS

SEE THE BIG PICTURE

WAIT TO ADD DETAILS UNTIL YOU ARE HAPPY WITH THE BASIC SHAPE OF YOUR DRAWING. YOU DON'T WANT TO SPEND TIME DETAILING A PART OF YOUR DRAWING THAT WILL BE ERASED LATER.

4

ROUND THE WINGTIPS AND ENGINES

ADD THE COCKPIT AND PASSENGER WINDOWS

5

INK AND COLOR

THIS AIRBUS IS WHITE WITH A BLUE STRIPE. AIRBUSES OWNED BY DIFFERENT AIRLINES HAVE DIFFERENT DESIGNS.

15

Seaplane
Aquatic Aircraft

Who needs a runway when there is a river or lake nearby! Seaplanes are designed to take off from and land on bodies of water. Many people use them to get from place to place, especially in **remote** areas or the wilderness. Large seaplanes are sometimes used for search and rescue, although rough waves can make for a tough landing!

BREATHE EASY

DRAWING A DIFFICULT SHAPE OR LINE WILL BE EASIER TO DO IF YOU DON'T HOLD YOUR BREATH!

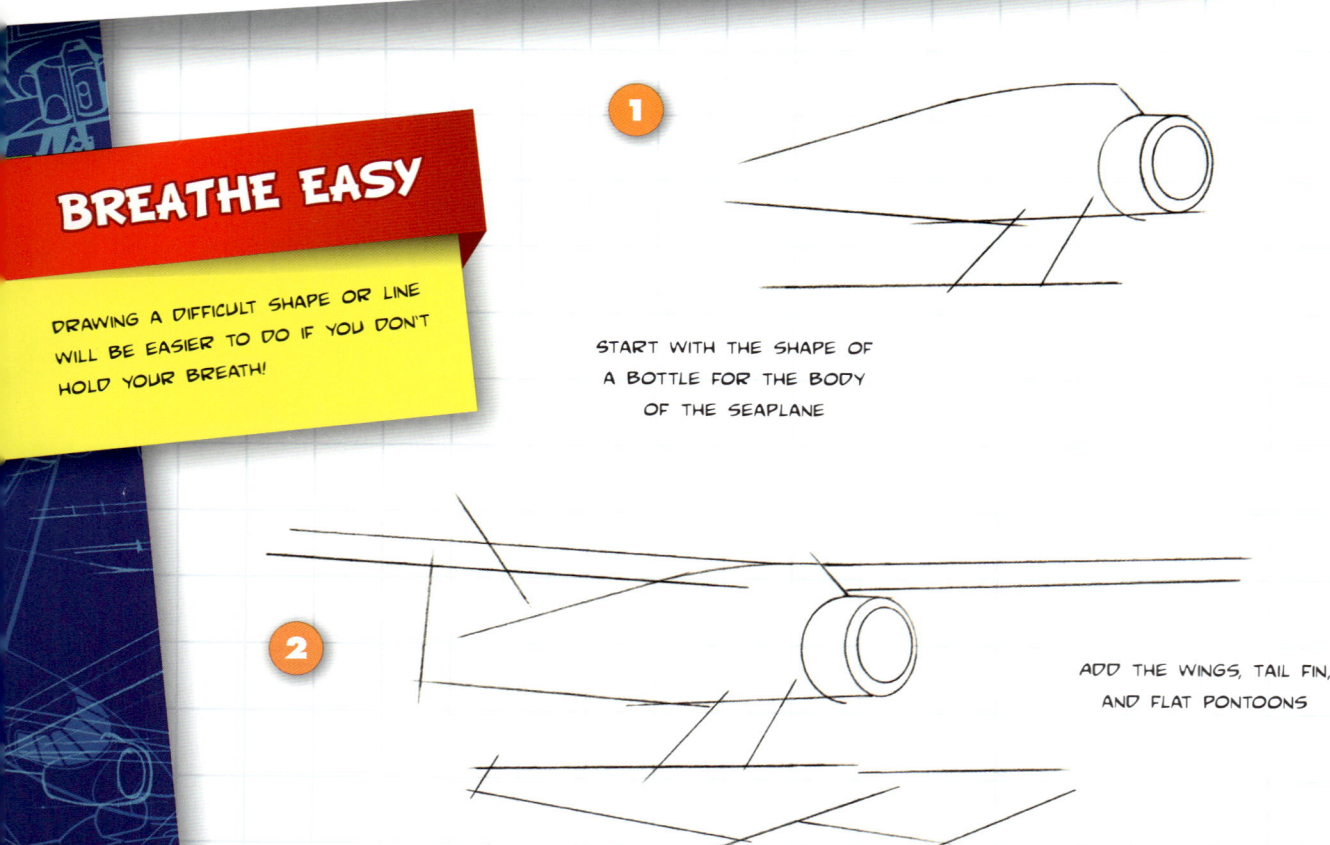

1. START WITH THE SHAPE OF A BOTTLE FOR THE BODY OF THE SEAPLANE

2. ADD THE WINGS, TAIL FIN, AND FLAT PONTOONS

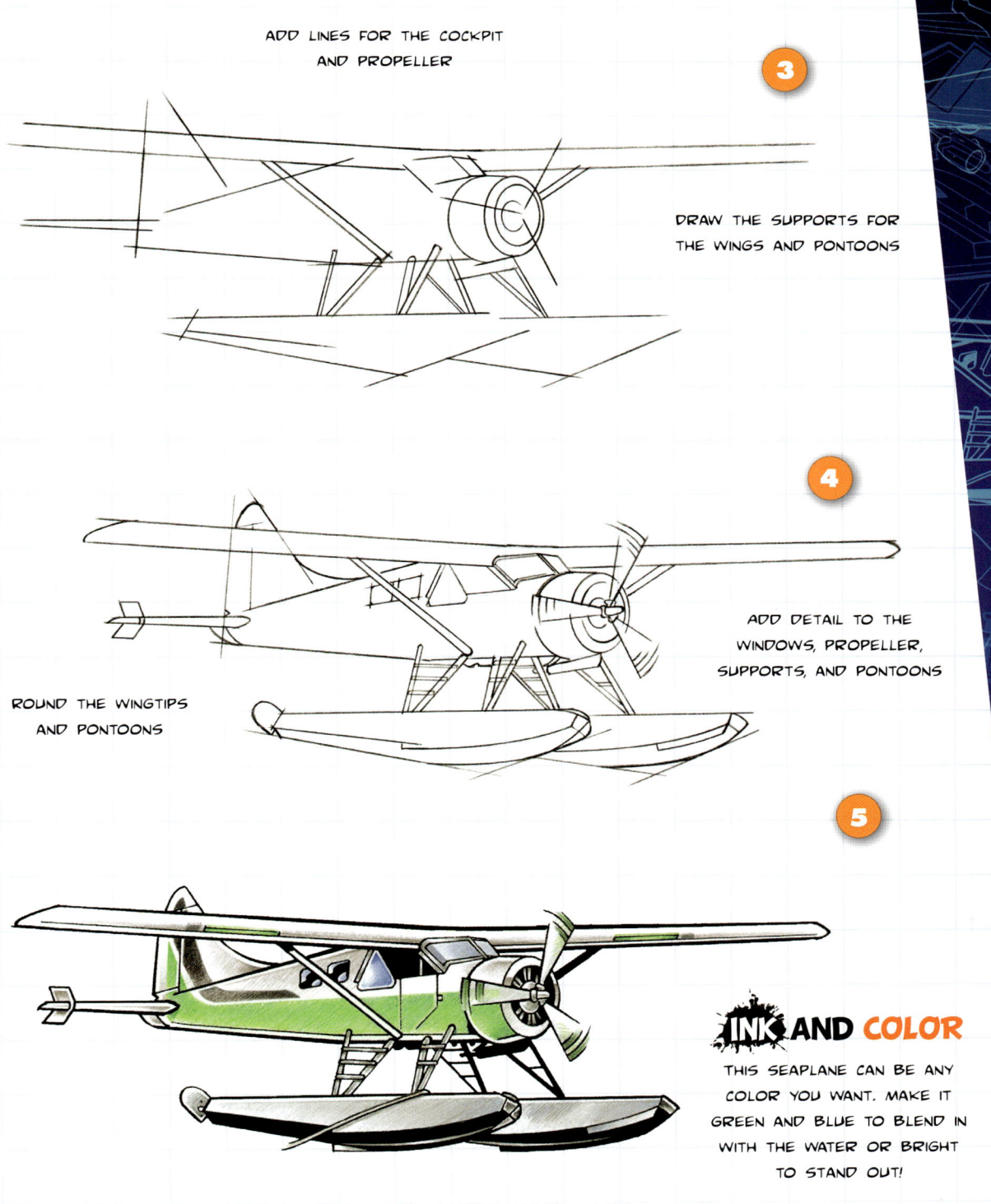

Learjet
Global Traveler

For over 50 years, Learjets have been used to transport business and military personnel around the world. Developed from a Swiss jet fighter, the original Learjet could seat six to eight people. Since then, several different models have been developed as technology has improved. A Learjet once flew across the United States in just over four hours.

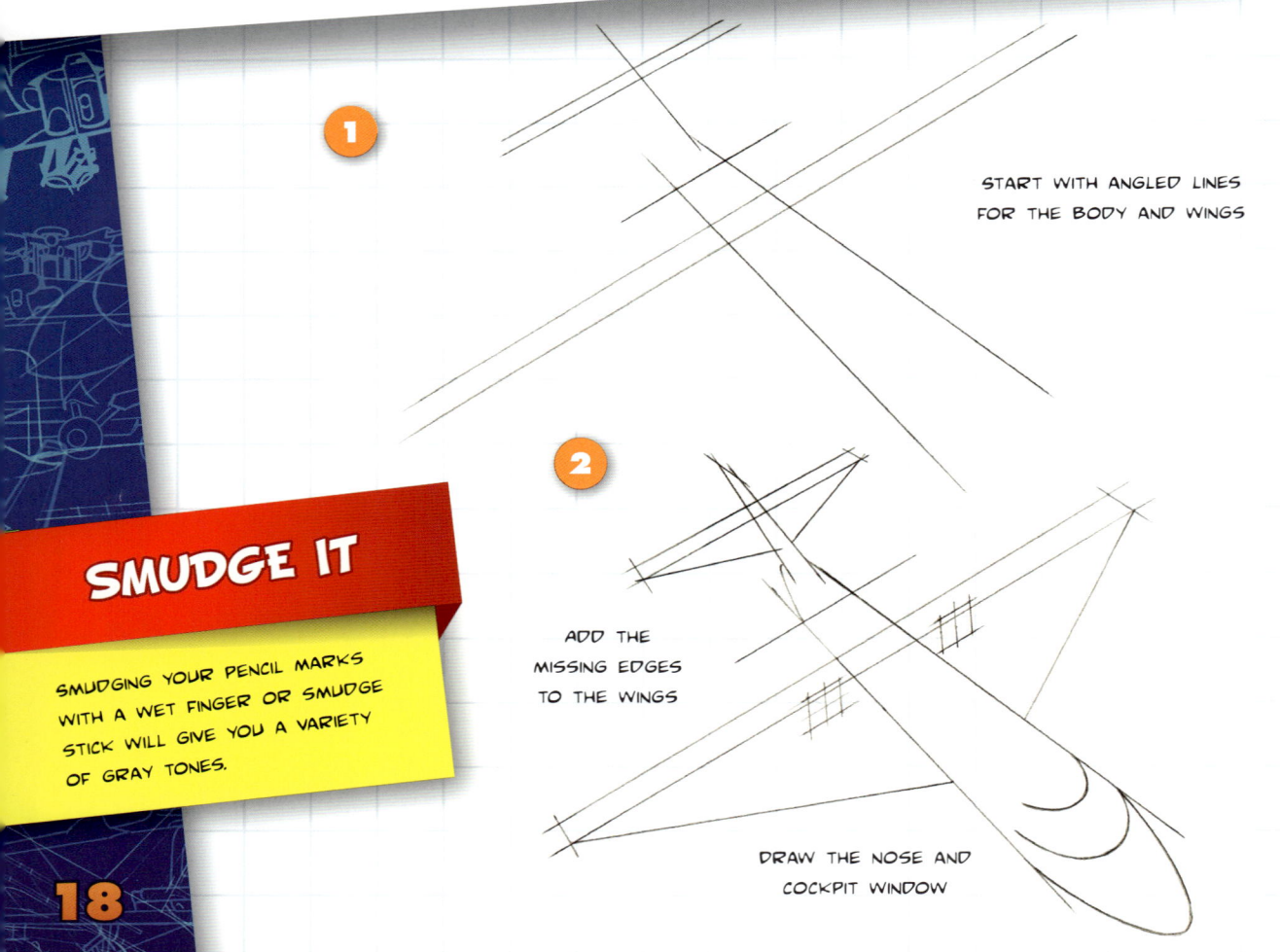

1. START WITH ANGLED LINES FOR THE BODY AND WINGS

2. ADD THE MISSING EDGES TO THE WINGS

DRAW THE NOSE AND COCKPIT WINDOW

SMUDGE IT

SMUDGING YOUR PENCIL MARKS WITH A WET FINGER OR SMUDGE STICK WILL GIVE YOU A VARIETY OF GRAY TONES.

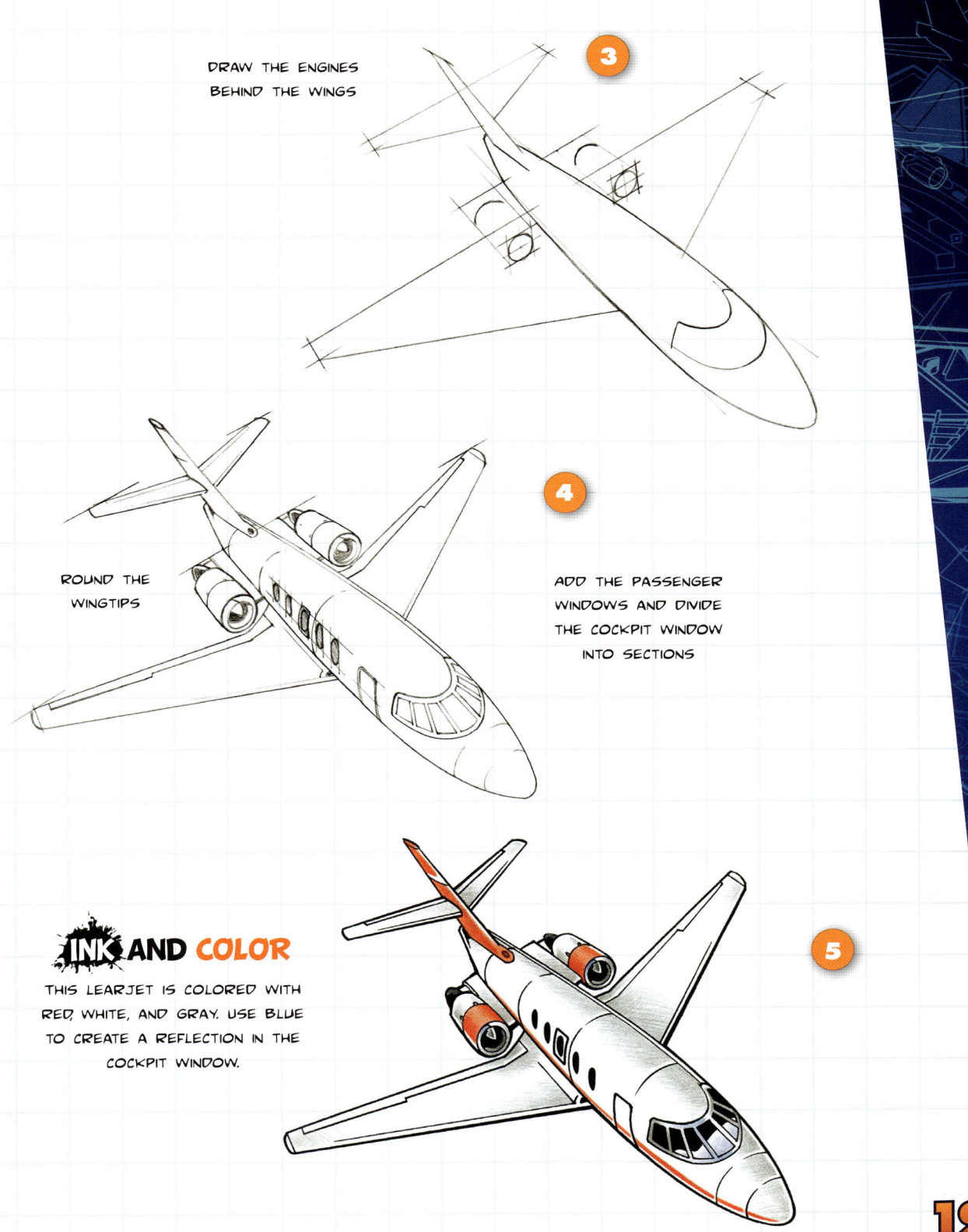

Apache Helicopter
Enemy Attacker

When enemy tanks are in the area, Apache helicopters get the call. These attack helicopters use missiles, **rockets**, and machine guns to destroy vehicles and buildings. Apaches are a critical part of the **armed forces** in countries around the globe.

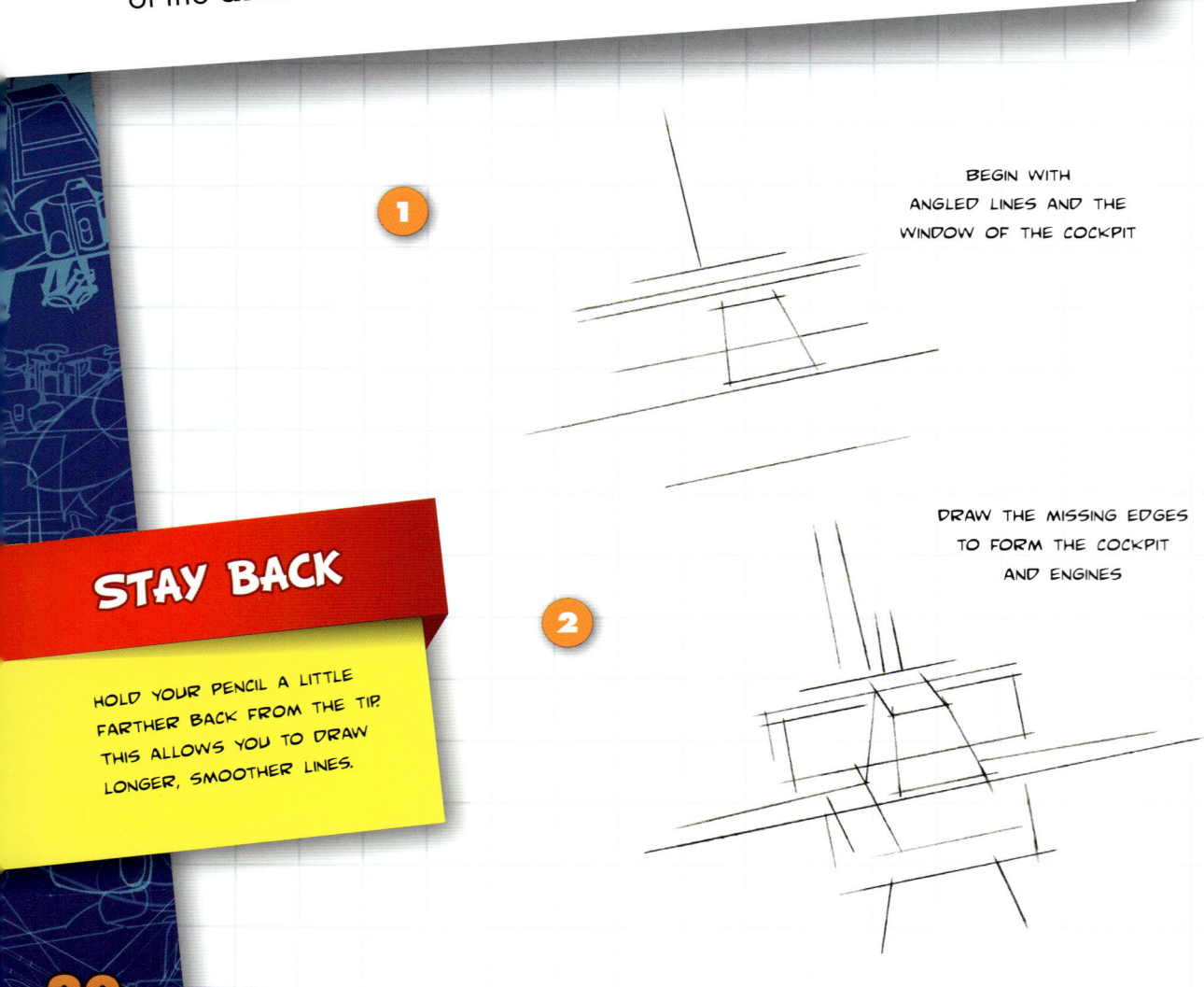

1. BEGIN WITH ANGLED LINES AND THE WINDOW OF THE COCKPIT

2. DRAW THE MISSING EDGES TO FORM THE COCKPIT AND ENGINES

STAY BACK

HOLD YOUR PENCIL A LITTLE FARTHER BACK FROM THE TIP. THIS ALLOWS YOU TO DRAW LONGER, SMOOTHER LINES.

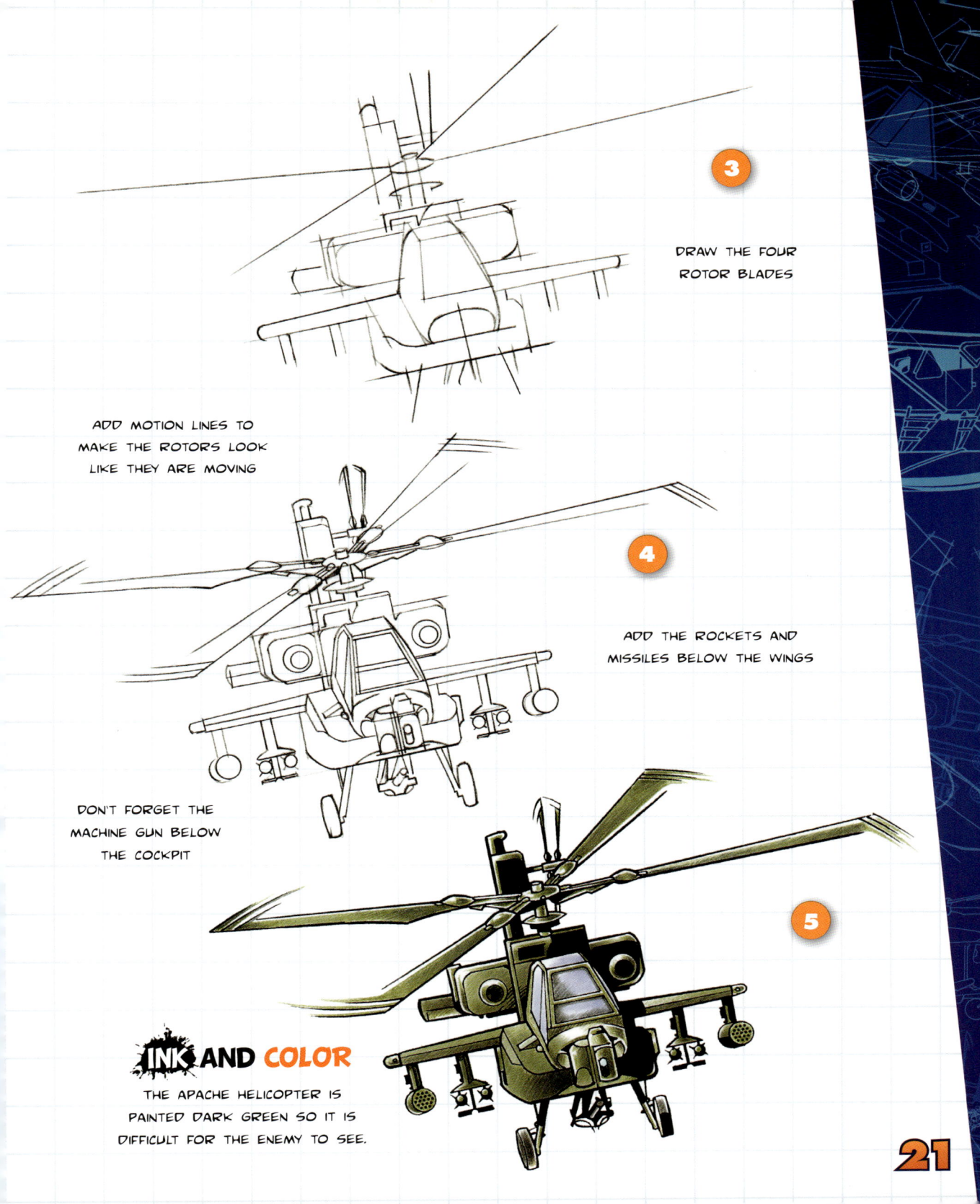

GLOSSARY

aerobatics—the performing of stunts and maneuvers by aircraft

armed forces—the military defense and fighting forces of a country

dogfight—the close combat between fighter planes

gates—the spaces that airplanes pull into for passenger boarding at airports

hoist—a giant reel used to lift people to safety

maneuverable—capable of changing position or direction quickly and easily

missiles—flying explosives that are guided to a target

passenger airliner—an airplane used to transport passengers

radar—a system that uses radio waves to locate targets

recon—a type of mission that involves gathering information about the enemy

remote—far removed from human development

rockets—flying explosives that are not guided

stealth—an aircraft's ability to fly without being spotted by radar

TO LEARN MORE

At the Library
LaPadula, Tom. *Learn to Draw Planes, Choppers & Watercraft.* Irvine, Calif.: Walter Foster Publishing, 2011.

Priceman, Marjorie. *Hot Air: The (Mostly) True Story of the First Hot-Air Balloon Ride.* New York, N.Y.: Atheneum Books for Young Readers, 2005.

Rinard, Judith. *The Story of Flight.* Toronto, Ont.: Firefly Books, 2002.

On the Web
Learning more about aircraft is as easy as 1, 2, 3.

1. Go to www.factsurfer.com.

2. Enter "aircraft" into the search box.

3. Click the "Surf" button and you will see a list of related Web sites.

With factsurfer.com, finding more information is just a click away.

INDEX

adding details, 15
Airbus A380, 14-15
Apache helicopter, 20-21
breathing, 16
drawing from photos, 4
drawing lightly, 5, 8
F-22 Raptor, 6-7
holding the pencil, 20
hot air balloon, 10-11
Jayhawk helicopter, 8-9
Learjet, 18-19
seaplane, 16-17
smudging, 5, 18
stunt plane, 12-13
supplies, 5
testing colors, 11
using basic shapes, 6
using your arm, 12